Quite simply, Parmigiano-Reggiano is one of the world's three or four incomparable cheeses. Its uniqueness has been recognized far beyond Italy's borders for over seven centuries. Never has an imitation equaled it. Eating a superb Parmigiano-Reggiano borders on privilege; there is grandeur in this cheese, and delight. Pure pleasure is breaking off a shard and letting it turn creamy and crackly on the tongue. Although fascinating to many, comprehending every detail of its production is not necessary. We all know greatness when we encounter it.

The secrets of Parmigiano-Reggiano's quality are found in its inconsistencies. In a world of mass-produced sameness, this cheese is made by hand, usually only eight or twelve wheels at a time. Topography also plays a role. Although the cheese can be made only within its legally designated zone in northern Italy, cheeses from the hills and cheeses from the plains are never quite alike.

Each cheese maker brings an individual philosophy to his cheeses, a philosophy developed over a decade of apprenticeship and then a lifetime of making Parmigiano-Reggiano every morning. Like exceptional music and art, Parmigiano-Reggiano celebrates the individual. Unlike music and art, this is greatness we can eat. Organizing this book by season is utterly logical when you know how significant seasons are to what appears on Italy's tables. The fresh, direct flavors of Italian food depend on each season's different flavors and textures: the peas of spring, crisp and sweet; summer's tomatoes, full-ripe and sensuous; autumn pears with their spicy juices; and rich velvety dairy products in winter.

Few people understand Parmigiano-Reggiano as does author Nancy Radke who has served as U.S. Director of Communications for the Consorzio del Formaggio Parmigiano-Reggiano since 1990. As a food professional who has lived in Italy, she developed a deep understanding of Italian culture. Nancy brings to these pages ways of enjoying Parmigiano-Reggiano that embrace its evolution through the seasons and centuries. Her recipes respect tradition, innovation, and always the integrity of the cheese. This is not the work of an author looking for another gimmick. It is the work of an authority impassioned with and immersed in the soul of one of the western world's extraordinary foods.

Lynne Rossetto Kasper

There's only one Parmigiano-Reggiano® – A cheese for all seasons. And it begins here.

Parmigiano-Reggiano is the world's unique parmesan, made from special ingredients found only one place on earth. It is handcrafted by artisans from a recipe over seven centuries old and aged slowly in carefully tended storehouses. The result of the cheese maker's passion is nothing less than extraordinary parmesan cheese. A cheese with rich, fruity flavor and a flaky, slightly grainy texture. A cheese that's nutritious and easy to digest. A cheese that is truly a

masterpiece. This is the homeland of Parmigiano-Reggiano—a region of northern Italy consisting largely of the counties of Reggio Emilia, Parma and Modena; Bologna (west of the Reno River); and Mantua (east of the Po River). Only here do the perfect conditions exist to make Parmigiano-Reggiano. The soil, the climate, the geography... all come together to produce especially flavorful, nutritious grasses which, in turn, yield a quality of milk found nowhere else.

Made by Hand... Seasoned with Time... A 900-Year-Old Tradition Endures

Dotting the hills and valleys of Parmigiano-Reggiano's controlled district are nearly 10,000 dairies that supply the milk for Parmigiano-Reggiano, and about 500 cheese houses where the prized wheels of parmesan are made. In each small family-owned cheese house or large *caseificio*, the process used to make Parmigiano-Reggiano has been handed down from generation to generation, and is much the same as it was over 900 years ago.

A Visit to a *Caseificio*

The traditional method of making Parmigiano-Reggiano begins with milk from two consecutive milkings—evening and morning. The evening milk is left overnight to separate naturally, after which a portion of the cream is skimmed off. The partially skimmed milk is mixed with the morning's whole milk, then poured into large copper kettles. Fermenting whey from the previous day's production is added, and the mixture is heated and stirred slowly. When the proper temperature is reached, calf's rennet (a natural extract) is added. After just a few moments, coagulation begins. The coagulated milk is the cheese

curd, the leftover liquid is the whey. A long-handled whisk is used to break the curd into fragments the size of wheat grains and, once again, the curd is heated and stirred until it reaches precise temperatures. The heat is then shut off and the curd is allowed to set while the granules form a solid mass in the bottom of the kettle. This mass is raised with a wooden paddle and cut into two pieces. Each piece is then wrapped in cheesecloth and placed in a circular wooden mold. After a few hours, the cheesecloth is removed and a special stamp is inserted between the cheese and the inside of the mold. This stamp forms a series of impressions around the sides of the wheel marking it with the number of the *caseificio*, the production month and year and the pin dots that form the words Parmigiano-Reggiano®. After resting for a few days, the cheese is immersed in brine for 20 to

25 days, then briefly exposed to the sun before being taken to the rooms where Parmi-giano-Reggiano is aged.

The Final Ingredient—Time

What makes Parmigiano-Reggiano so outstanding is its long and careful aging. Each wheel of Parmigiano-Reggiano is aged for an average of 24 months—the longest of any hard cheese. During the aging process, important changes take place that give Parmigiano-Reggiano its distinctive flavor, texture, aroma and nutritional value.

The Seasons Play an Important Role

In the climate-sensitive aging rooms, the wheels of Parmigiano-Reggiano rest on specially designed wooden shelves. During the warm summers, butterfat rises to the surface of the wheel. In winter, it remains deep inside. Consequently, cheeses made in the winter tend to be higher in butterfat and softer, ideal for serving as a table cheese, while summer cheeses are drier and better for grating. But perhaps the most important change that takes place during the aging process is the breakdown of Parmigiano-Reggiano's milk protein. As the cheese ages, peptones, peptides and free amino acids begin to form. When the free amino acids crystallize, they give Parmigiano-Reggiano its distinctive, slightly crunchy texture. They also make Parmigiano-Reggiano easier to digest... and a perfect source of quick energy.

The Oval Brand—A Mark of Good Taste

After the wheels of Parmigiano-Reggiano have aged for one year, professional cheese testers scrutinize each one, evaluating many different attributes: maturation, aroma, color, consistency and internal structure. When the tester is satisfied, the wheel is branded with the Tutela Consorzio Parmigiano-Reggiano® oval and left to finish aging. After approximately six more months, the wheels are tested again and those of the highest quality are branded with the Export® firebrand. They are now ready for shipment around the world.

Keeping Parmigiano-Reggiano Fresh

Once a wheel has been opened and exposed to air, Parmigiano-Reggiano becomes susceptible to oxidation. This chemical reaction causes the cheese to become dried out, robbing it of flavor and aroma. To minimize flavor loss, keep wedges tightly wrapped in plastic wrap. Then remember that every time the cheese is used it should be rewrapped in new plastic wrap to achieve a tight seal. Keep grated Parmigiano-Reggiano in a plastic zip-style bag that has had all the air pressed out of it. Store cheese in the warmest part of the refrigerator at approximately 40° F(4° C). There is no need to ever freeze Parmigiano-Reggiano. This will damage its texture and ruin its flavor.

The Right Cheese for a Healthy Diet
Any Time of the Year

Today's health-conscious individual often thinks cheese—especially one as luscious as Parmigiano-Reggiano—has no place in a healthy diet. But nothing could be further from the truth. In fact, Parmigiano-Reggiano's high-quality ingredients, all-natural production methods and long aging all combine to make this cheese nutritious fare for anyone, young or old.

Packed with Vitamins and Minerals

It takes an amazing 160 gallons (605 liters) of high-quality milk to make one 85-pound (39 kg) wheel of Parmigiano-Reggiano. Thanks to impeccable handling and production standards—adhered to in all Parmigiano-Reggiano dairies and cheese houses—this milk requires none of the sterilization procedures that can damage milk's delicate nutrients. As a result, each pound (455 g) of Parmigiano-Reggiano contains the concentrated nutrients of two gallons (7.5 liters) of milk. An excellent source of protein, calcium and phosphorous, the cheese is rich in vitamins A, B2, B6, B12, E, D and K; pantothenic acid, biotin, magnesium, zinc, copper, potassium, sodium and cobalt. Actually, Parmigiano-Reggiano has more vitamins and minerals than most other sources of animal protein—a real plus for those limiting their meat consumption. It not only contains 18 of the body's 21 required amino acids, but it is an exceptional source of B12, a vitamin lacking in most vegetarian diets.

Lower in Fat and Sodium

Because Parmigiano-Reggiano is made from part-skim cow's milk, it's one of the lowest in fat and cholesterol of any aged natural cheese. One flavor-packed tablespoon (5 g) grated over pasta, risotto, salad or soup adds a host of vitamins and minerals but only 1.5 grams of fat and 4 milligrams of cholesterol. Anyone concerned about salt intake will be happy to learn that, at 30 milligrams per tablespoon (5 g), Parmigiano-Reggiano contains one-third the sodium found in other hard grating cheeses produced in Europe and North and South America.

Easier to Digest

During Parmigiano-Reggiano's long and careful aging, its milk protein breaks down into free amino acids. This natural process not only gives the cheese its distinctive crunch, it makes Parmigiano-Reggiano remarkably easy to digest.

Compared to other animal proteins which take four hours to assimilate, Parmigiano-Reggiano is digested in just 45 minutes. That's why Italian athletes include this cheese in their post workout diet—it's a quick way to replenish lost nutrients. Still, athletes aren't the only ones to benefit from Parmigiano-Reggiano's easy digestibility. Babies who eat it sprinkled on rice cereal, children, adults, the elderly—even people who are lactose intolerant—can enjoy Parmigiano-Reggiano.

Spring

emerges in mid-March filling every inch of fertile earth with lush grasses tipped with dancing yellow flowers.
It's a veritable feast for the cows whose diet in this season is rich and varied.
This produces milk tinted a delicate yellow from the carotene in the wild spring flowers which also lend their hue and aroma to the wheels of parmesan made in March, April and May.

Crostini with Sweet Peas and Bitter Greens

Crostini primavera

10 ounces fresh or frozen baby peas (280 g)
1/4 teaspoon salt
4 ounces PARMIGIANO-REGGIANO (113 g)
24 slices crusty baguette
2 cloves garlic, peeled
Extra-virgin olive oil
4 ounces fresh young arugula leaves, cleaned (113 g)
24 large mint leaves, cleaned
Aged balsamic vinegar
Black pepper to grind

ℰ

Blanch peas until tender in boiling water (2–4 minutes for fresh, 1 minute for frozen). Drain and pat dry. Puree in a food processor with salt. Set aside.

Make 1 cup (113 g) of Parmigiano-Reggiano slivers with a vegetable peeler. Toast bread until golden on both sides. Rub lightly with garlic, and brush with olive oil.

To assemble crostini, spread toast with pea puree, top with arugula and a mint leaf. Sprinkle with balsamic vinegar. Top with Parmigiano-Reggiano slivers and pepper.
Serves 8

Spinach and Ricotta Dumplings

Gnocchi di spinaci e ricotta

40 ounces fresh spinach, washed (1150 g)
16 ounces ricotta cheese (455 g)
1 1/2 cups freshly grated
PARMIGIANO-REGGIANO, divided (120 g)
1 teaspoon salt (6 g)
1/2 teaspoon pepper
1/4 teaspoon nutmeg
2 extra-large eggs, slightly beaten
Flour
8 tablespoons unsalted butter (113 g)
1 teaspoon sage (1 g)
1/4 teaspoon salt

Cook spinach until limp, drain and cool. Squeeze by handfuls until bone dry. Chop finely. Turn ricotta out onto paper towels. Pat dry. Mix together in large bowl with spinach, 1 cup (80 g) of Parmigiano-Reggiano, salt, pepper, nutmeg and eggs. Refrigerate 15 minutes.

Drop spinach-ricotta mixture by level tablespoons onto a floured work surface. Roll one at a time in your hands into fat, neat cylinders. Place on a floured cutting board (May be prepared ahead to this point—cover with a tea towel and refrigerate).

Melt together butter, sage and salt. Coat bottom of a serving dish with half the butter mixture and 1/4 cup (20 g) of Parmigiano-Reggiano. Keep warm in a very low oven.

Gently drop a dozen dumplings into a large quantity of well-salted simmering water. Dumplings are cooked when they rise to the surface. Drain with a slotted spoon, transfer to the serving dish. Finish dish with remaining sage-butter and Parmigiano-Reggiano. Serve with more Parmigiano-Reggiano at the table. *Serves 4*

Baked Asparagus

Asparagi al forno

1 pound asparagus, washed, tough bottoms snapped off (455 g)
1 tablespoon olive oil (15 ml)
Salt and freshly ground pepper
1 ounce PARMIGIANO-REGGIANO slivers (28 g)
1 teaspoon aged balsamic vinegar (5 ml)

Preheat oven to 400° F (200° C). Place asparagus and olive oil in a large baking dish, roll until evenly coated. Arrange in a single layer. Season with salt and freshly ground pepper. Cover with foil, bake 12–15 minutes until asparagus is tender when pierced with knife tip. Remove from oven. (May be prepared ahead to this point)
Make 1/4 cup (28 g) of thin Parmigiano-Reggiano slivers with a vegetable peeler. Scatter slivers over asparagus and return the dish to the oven. Continue baking just until the cheese softens, about 2–3 minutes.
Place the asparagus on warmed plates and sprinkle with several drops of balsamic vinegar. Serve immediately.
Serves 4

Roman Egg-Drop Soup

Stracciatella alla romana

4 extra-large eggs
1/4 cup freshly grated PARMIGIANO-REGGIANO (20 g)
2 tablespoons fresh lemon juice (30 ml)
2 tablespoons chopped Italian parsley (8 g)
1/4 teaspoon nutmeg
1/2 teaspoon salt
2 quarts homemade chicken broth (2 liters)

Beat eggs in a small bowl until just blended. Add Parmigiano-Reggiano,
lemon juice, parsley, nutmeg and salt. Mix well.
Bring broth to a rolling boil in a saucepan. Pour in egg mixture, stirring
gently and constantly with a wire whisk. Reduce heat to a simmer.
Cook 2–3 minutes until egg mixture forms tiny flakes. Serve piping hot.
Serves 8

RX for Good Health

Probably more doctors in
Italy prescribe Parmigiano-
Reggiano than any other
food. Why? Because it is a
highly nutritious food in a
very easy to digest form. It
takes just 45 minutes for
the body to assimilate the
nutrients in Parmigiano-
Reggiano versus 4 hours for
other protein sources.

That means that a
sprinkling on baby's rice
cereal will add lots of
calcium, phosphorous and
vitamins without tying an
infant's delicate system up in
knots. Senior citizens and
people with all manner of
digestive problems are also
told to eat Parmigiano-
Reggiano to help sustain
their strength. In fact, the
17th century French
playwright Moliere was
convinced that it kept him
alive in his old age.

Spaghetti with Lemon

Spaghetti al limone

2–3 tablespoons coarse salt (12–18 g) • 1 pound spaghetti (455 g)
10 tablespoons unsalted butter (142 g) • 1 tablespoon lemon zest (18 g)
2 tablespoons lemon juice (30 ml) • 1/2 teaspoon salt
1/4 teaspoon black pepper • 1/3 cup packed fresh basil leaves, chopped (14 g)
3/4 cup freshly grated PARMIGIANO-REGGIANO (60 g)
6 sprigs fresh basil for garnish

Add coarse salt to 2 gallons (7.5 liters) of rapidly boiling water. Stir in spaghetti and cook until al dente. Drain.

Meanwhile, melt butter in a large sauté pan. Add zest, juice, salt and pepper. Heat gently 1 minute. Toss with spaghetti.

Add basil and Parmigiano-Reggiano and toss until spaghetti is evenly coated. Serve in warm pasta bowls and garnish. Sprinkle with more Parmigiano-Reggiano at the table.

Serves 6

Gilded Chicken Breasts

Petti di pollo dorati

3/4 cup pine nuts (64 g)
3/4 cup grated
PARMIGIANO-REGGIANO (60 g)
1 clove garlic
1/4 cup packed parsley leaves (28 g)
1 teaspoon rosemary (2 g)
8 boneless skinless half chicken breasts,
trimmed of all fat
8 teaspoons Dijon mustard (48 g)

℘

Toast pine nuts in a 300° F (150° C) oven until golden. Combine nuts and next four ingredients in a food processor and chop coarsely. Place in a large flat pan.
Brush top side of each chicken breast with 1 teaspoon (6 g) Dijon. Press mustard-coated side only into nut topping.

Arrange breasts, coated side up, on a lightly greased baking sheet. Sprinkle with remaining topping. Bake at 375° F (190° C) for 25–30 minutes, until light golden brown.
Serves 6-8

Summer

lies heavy on the land, hot and cloudless. The grasses become dry and concentrated. Cheeses made in summer are set out to begin their aging process on shelves in rooms as warm as the outside environment. As a result, they sweat butterfat rapidly as their tender new rinds form during the months of June, July and August. This makes the wheels of summer drier in texture and more pungent in flavor—the perfect cheeses for grating.

Tuscan Style Carpaccio
Carpaccio alla toscana

1 pound beef tenderloin (455 g) • 1 clove garlic, halved lengthwise
2 tablespoons lemon juice (30 ml) • 1 teaspoon Dijon mustard (6 g)
1/2 teaspoon salt • 6 tablespoons extra-virgin olive oil (90 ml)
Freshly ground black pepper • 3 ounces PARMIGIANO-REGGIANO (85 g)
1 small bunch arugula, washed

Trim all fat and membrane from meat and cover with plastic wrap. Partially freeze 2–3 hours until very firm, but not hard frozen. For each of 5 servings:
Slice meat across the grain 1/8"(0.3 cm) thick. Center 1 slice of beef on a large piece of plastic wrap; then arrange 4–6 slices around it like flower petals. (Slices may touch, not overlap) Cover with more wrap. Pound evenly and gently with a disk pounder. Meat should be translucent when held up to light. Rub a luncheon plate with garlic. Remove 1 sheet of plastic wrap from meat. Invert plate over meat, tuck plastic wrap over plate and flip plate upright. Keep covered and chilled. Repeat for remaining servings. Prepare sauce by whisking lemon juice, mustard and salt together in a bowl. Whisk in oil in a thin steady stream until a creamy vinaigrette is formed. Add pepper. Set aside. Just before serving, make thin shavings of Parmigiano-Reggiano with a vegetable peeler. Remove plastic wrap from meat, season with freshly ground pepper, drizzle with 1/2 the vinaigrette. Arrange arugula and Parmigiano-Reggiano evenly over each portion. Finish with the remaining vinaigrette. *Serves 5*

Radicchio Soup

Acquacotta di radicchio

1 pound radicchio (455 g)
3 tablespoons + 1/4 cup olive oil, divided (45 + 60 ml)
1 large clove garlic, chopped • 1 small red onion, chopped
1 15-ounce can tomato sauce (425 g)
3 cups water (700 ml) • Salt and pepper to taste
4 cups cubed crusty Italian bread (225 g)
3/4 cup freshly grated PARMIGIANO-REGGIANO (60 g)
1/3 cup fresh basil leaves (14 g)

Wash radicchio, quarter and remove cores. Chop coarsely. Place 3 tablespoons (45 ml) of olive oil, garlic, onion and radicchio in a soup kettle. Set over medium heat and sauté 10 minutes until softened.

Add tomato sauce and water. Season with salt and pepper. Bring to a simmer and cook gently for 5 minutes. Meanwhile, toss bread cubes with the remaining 1/4 cup (60 ml) olive oil. Sauté in a large pan set over medium-high heat until cubes are golden, turning them frequently. (Make ahead to this point) Heat soup. Add Parmigiano-Reggiano and basil and stir until cheese melts. Place bread cubes in the bottom of 4 soup bowls. Pour the soup over the bread. Serve immediately with more Parmigiano-Reggiano at the table. *Serves 4*

Portabello Mushroom Sandwich

Panino ai funghi

3 large yellow peppers

6 large Portabello mushroom caps, brushed clean, stems removed

Extra-virgin olive oil

Aged balsamic vinegar

4 ounce mixed field salad, cleaned (113 g)

6 4"-squares of focaccia, sliced in half (10 cm)

24 whole basil leaves

1 recipe Savory PARMIGIANO-REGGIANO Spread

Broil peppers until their skins blacken and blister, about 4-5 minutes on each side.

Place peppers in a brown bag and let set 10 minutes to steam skins loose. Remove skins and seeds; cut peppers into halves.

Brush mushrooms with olive oil and grill over high heat. Turn as necessary, grilling until tender.

Sprinkle with a bit of balsamic vinegar.

Place a small handful of greens on the bottom half of each piece of focaccia. Top with a mushroom and half of a roasted pepper. Add 4 basil leaves to each sandwich. Smear a generous dollop of Savory Parmigiano-Reggiano Spread on the top slice of focaccia and press sandwich firmly together. *Serves 6*

Savory Parmigiano-Reggiano Spread

Maionese al Parmigiano-Reggiano

13 3/4-ounce can of water-packed artichoke hearts (390 g)

1 cup mayonnaise (225 g)

1 cup grated PARMIGIANO-REGGIANO (80 g)

Drain artichoke hearts and chop into small pieces. In a small bowl stir together artichokes, mayonnaise and Parmigiano-Reggiano. Cover and refrigerate until needed. *Makes 3 cups*

Linguine with Prosciutto

Linguine al prosciutto

2 tablespoons olive oil (30 ml)
1/4 cup red onion, finely chopped (40 g)
1 teaspoon salt (6 g)
1 12-ounce can evaporated skimmed milk (354 ml)
1 teaspoon grated lemon zest (2 g)
3 ounces Prosciutto di Parma®, thinly sliced (85 g)
10 fresh basil leaves
1/4 cup fresh parsley leaves (15 g)
4 fresh mint leaves or 1/4 teaspoon dried
1 pound linguine (455 g)
3/4 cup freshly grated PARMIGIANO-REGGIANO (60 g)
Freshly ground pepper

Heat olive oil in a large sauté pan over medium. Add onion and salt. Sauté 5 minutes until onions soften. Add evaporated skimmed milk and the grated lemon zest. Cook 1 minute and remove from heat.

Cut Prosciutto into thin strips. Set aside. Combine basil, parsley and mint and chop finely. Set aside.

Cook linguine in rapidly boiling salted water. Just before the pasta is done, briefly return the sauté pan to medium heat and warm the sauce. When the pasta is al dente, drain and add to the sauté pan along with the herbs and the Parmigiano-Reggiano.

Toss the pasta until the cheese melts and a light sauce forms. Add Prosciutto, season with freshly ground pepper to taste and toss briefly. Serve immediately in warm pasta bowls with more Parmigiano-Reggiano at the table. *Serves 4-6*

Penne with Raw Tomato Sauce

Penne alla salsa cruda di pomodoro

1 pound Italian plum tomatoes (455 g)
3 ounces PARMIGIANO-REGGIANO (85 g)
3 ounces fresh arugula (85 g)
1/3 cup extra-virgin olive oil (80 ml)
1 teaspoon minced garlic (3 g)
16 leaves fresh basil, torn
1 teaspoon salt (6 g)
1 tablespoon aged balsamic vinegar (15 ml)
1 pound penne (455 g)

Bring 2 gallons (7.5 liters) of water to a boil. Drop in tomatoes; then remove after 30–45 seconds. Save water to cook pasta. Peel tomatoes and remove core. Cut tomatoes around their equators and squeeze out seeds. Dice tomato flesh into 1/2" (1.25 cm) pieces and place in a large pasta bowl.

With a vegetable peeler make thick shavings of Parmigiano-Reggiano. When the cheese gets too small to shave, grate the rest. Put the grated cheese and 1/2 the shavings into the bowl along with the tomatoes. Wash and stem arugula leaves. Dry and tear into small pieces. Add to bowl along with remaining ingredients except the pasta. Toss well.

Add 2–3 tablespoons salt (12–18 g) to the boiling pasta water. Cook pasta until al dente. Drain and immediately toss pasta with the sauce until well coated. Serve in pasta bowls and shower each with the remaining slivers of Parmigiano-Reggiano. Add freshly ground pepper at the table. *Serves 6*

Baked Layered Eggplant

Melanzane in tortiera

5 pounds eggplant (2270 g)
1/2 cup olive oil (118 ml) or olive oil spray
Salt
1 1/2 pounds fresh Italian plum tomatoes (685 g)
1 medium red onion, chopped • 1 large clove garlic, chopped
1 1/2 teaspoons marjoram (1.5 g)
6 tablespoons unsalted butter (85 g)
8 tablespoons flour (56 g)
3 cups milk (700 ml)
1/2 teaspoon pepper • 1/2 teaspoon nutmeg
1 1/2 cups grated PARMIGIANO-REGGIANO, divided (120 g)
1/2 pound Fontina or Bel Paese cheese, shredded (225 g)

Wash and peel eggplant. Slice 1/2″ (1.25 cm) thick. Preheat broiler. Brush or spray several baking pans lightly with olive oil. Cover with a single layer of eggplant. Brush or spray slices lightly with oil. Broil 7″ (18 cm) from heat, until deep golden brown, about 6–10 minutes. Watch carefully. Turn pieces and broil another 5 minutes. Season with salt and set aside.

Cut tomatoes in half around their equators. Remove seeds. Place cut sides against a coarse grater and grate pulp; then discard skins. Cook onion and garlic 6–7 minutes in 2 tablespoons (30 ml) olive oil until soft. Add tomatoes, marjoram and 1/2 teaspoon salt. Simmer 10 minutes until reduced and very thick.

Prepare béchamel sauce by melting butter in a small saucepan. Whisk in flour all at once and cook 1–2 minutes, stirring frequently. Add milk, whisking constantly. Bring to a boil. Reduce heat and simmer, whisking constantly, 2 minutes. Remove from heat and season with pepper, nutmeg and 1/2 cup (40 g) of Parmigiano-Reggiano. Set aside.

Grease bottom and sides of a 9x13″ (23x36 cm) baking dish. Layer in 1/3 of the eggplant slices. Spread 1/3 of the béchamel sauce thinly over the eggplant. Dot with 1/3 of the thickened tomato sauce. Sprinkle with 1/3 of the shredded cheese and 5 tablespoons (24 g) Parmigiano-Reggiano. Repeat for two more layers. (Can make ahead and refrigerate)

Preheat oven to 350° F (177° C). Bake 30 minutes (45 if refrigerated); then broil top until lightly browned. Remove from oven and let set 10–15 minutes before serving. Cut into squares and serve immediately.
Serves 8-12

Autumn

bathes the ground with cooling rains. A new flush of grasses and wild flowers emerges. Once again the cows' diet is fragrantly varied. The natural casein level in the milk is also at its highest. This means that cheeses made in September, October and November have the greatest potential for long aging, and for flavor and aroma development. Balanced and polished, autumn Parmigiano-Reggiano makes a perfect table cheese.

Two Potato Tart

Torta di patate

4 ounces PARMIGIANO-REGGIANO (113 g)
1 pound sweet potatoes, peeled (455 g)
1 pound all-purpose potatoes, peeled (455 g)
2 tablespoons unsalted butter (28 g) • 2 tablespoons olive oil (30 ml)
Salt and pepper • Freshly grated nutmeg

Make 1 cup (113 g) of Parmigiano-Reggiano slivers with a vegetable peeler. Set aside. Slice the potatoes very thinly, sweet potatoes first, then all-purpose. As soon as potatoes are sliced, melt butter and olive oil together in a small pan. Pour half into a 9″ (23 cm) cast iron skillet set over low heat.

Make a layer using 1/3 of the white potato slices, overlapping them in the bottom of the skillet, circling in a spiral from the outside edge to the center. Sprinkle lightly with salt, pepper and nutmeg. Scatter 1/5 of the Parmigiano-Reggiano slivers over the layer.

Next make a layer using 1/3 of the sweet potatoes, overlapping them in a spiral going in the opposite direction. Season and scatter with Parmigiano-Reggiano slivers. Continue making layers of potato slices, seasonings and cheese. The 6th and final layer will be of sweet potatoes. Season and pour remaining melted butter and oil over the top.

Cover pan tightly with foil, crimping edges to seal. Bake in a preheated 425° F (220° C) oven for 25 minutes. Remove foil and continue cooking 25 minutes, until potatoes are tender and browned at the edges. Cut into wedges and serve immediately. *Serves 6*

Butternut Squash Risotto

Risotto alla zucca

4 tablespoons unsalted butter (57 g)
2 cups winter squash or pumpkin,
peeled, seeded and diced (275 g)
3/4 cup onion, finely chopped (85 g)
1 3/4 cups Arborio rice (370 g)
1/2 cup white wine (125 ml)
6 cups chicken broth, simmering (1.5 liter)
1 cup freshly grated
PARMIGIANO-REGGIANO (80 g)
1 tablespoon finely chopped sage (3 g)
2 tablespoons chopped parsley (6 g)

Slowly melt butter in a large sauté pan over medium-low heat. Add squash and onion. Sauté gently 5 minutes, until onion becomes translucent. Add rice and continue to cook over medium heat, stirring constantly until rice looks opaque, 6–8 minutes. Pour in wine and simmer until the liquid evaporates.

Add 1/2 of the simmering broth all at once to the rice. Raise heat so that the liquid bubbles over the entire surface. Cook the rice a total of 18 minutes from this point, stirring often. As the rice absorbs the broth, add some more, a little at a time. Be careful not to add too much broth at the end of the cooking time because the rice should be naturally creamy, not swimming in broth or fluffy and dry.

Stir in the Parmigiano-Reggiano and the sage. Remove from heat, cover and let stand several minutes. Stir in parsley and serve with more grated Parmigiano-Reggiano at the table. *Serves 4-6*

Parmigiano-Reggiano "Ice Cream"

"Gelato" di Parmigiano-Reggiano

1 cup heavy cream (237 ml)
2 cloves garlic, peeled and sliced in half lengthwise
1/4 teaspoon nutmeg
2 cups grated PARMIGIANO-REGGIANO (160 g)
Aged balsamic vinegar, the older the better

Accompaniments:

Multigrain raisin or crusty French bread
Red grapes
Pear or apple slices
Walnuts
Spicy greens such as arugula

Bring cream, garlic and nutmeg to a boil in a heavy saucepan over medium-high heat, watching constantly. Remove garlic from the cream. Add Parmigiano-Reggiano, 1/2 cup (40 g) at a time, stirring constantly until all the cheese is incorporated.

Continue stirring until cheese is melted, about 1 minute. Remove from heat, pour into a shallow heat-resistant dish and cool to room temperature. Cover dish and refrigerate until cheese stiffens.

Scoop portions of "gelato" with an ice cream scoop onto 6 salad plates.

Garnish with your choice of accompaniments listed above. Drip a few drops of aged balsamic vinegar over the "gelato" and serve. *Serves 6*

Sausage and White Bean Stew

Salsicce e fagioli in umido

12 ounces dried baby lima beans (340 g)
1/4 pound pancetta (113 g)
1 stalk celery • 1 carrot • 1 medium onion
9 large cloves peeled garlic, divided
1 28-ounce can Italian plum tomatoes (794 g)
2 tablespoons olive oil (30 ml)
6 links Italian poultry sausage (683 g)
4 ounces PARMIGIANO-REGGIANO rinds (113 g)
1 pound peeled and cubed butternut squash (455 g)
1 teaspoon sage (1 g)
1 1/2 teaspoons rosemary (3 g)
1/4 cup flour (28 g)
3 cups chicken broth (354 ml)
Salt and pepper to taste
20 ounces cooked spinach, drained (567 g)

Pick over beans, discarding shriveled ones. Place in a bowl and cover with 4 cups (1 liter) water. Soak overnight.

Preheat oven to 325° F (163° C). Roughly chop together pancetta, celery, carrot, onion, and 1 clove of garlic. Drain tomatoes, reserving juice separately. Slice tomatoes and set everything aside.

Heat olive oil in a large sauté pan set over medium. Add sausages and brown, 2 minutes each side. Remove pan from heat and transfer sausages to the bottom of a 5-quart Dutch oven. Layer in rinds, drained beans, squash cubes, sliced tomatoes and remaining whole garlic cloves.

Place sauté pan back over medium. Add chopped ingredients, sage and rosemary. Cook until softened, 6–8 minutes. Sprinkle with flour and mix well. Add reserved tomato juice and chicken broth. Bring to a simmer. Season with salt and pepper. Pour contents of sauté pan over ingredients in the Dutch oven. Cover and bake 2 1/2 hours or until beans are tender.

Carefully remove cheese rinds and cut into small cubes. Return cubes to stew and stir gently. Divide cooked spinach among 6 soup bowls. Ladle a sausage and beans into each. Serve with additional grated Parmigiano-Reggiano at the table. *Serves 6*

Parmigiano-Reggiano, Mushroom and Celery Salad

Insalata di Parmigiano-Reggiano, funghi e sedano

2 tablespoons lemon juice (30 ml)
1/4 teaspoon salt • 1 teaspoon Dijon mustard (6 g)
4 tablespoons extra-virgin olive oil (60 ml)
1 teaspoon minced shallot • Freshly ground pepper
1 pound fresh mushrooms, cleaned (455 g)
6 ounces celery hearts (170 g)
2 teaspoons chopped fresh parsley • 2 teaspoons chopped fresh mint
4 ounces PARMIGIANO-REGGIANO (113 g)
6 lettuce leaves

Whisk together lemon juice, salt and mustard, until salt dissolves. Add oil in a very thin stream, whisking constantly. Stir in shallots and ground pepper.

Thinly slice mushrooms through cap and stem. Slice celery thinly on an angle. Combine mushrooms, celery, parsley and mint in a large bowl. With a vegetable peeler, sliver 1/2 of the Parmigiano-Reggiano over the top. (Can be made ahead to this point and chilled)

Just before serving, place lettuce leaves on 6 plates. Toss salad with dressing and mound on each plate. Sliver remaining Parmigiano-Reggiano over each portion.

Serves 6

32

Minted Poached Pears

Pere cotte alla menta

2 cups water (570 ml) • 2 cups red wine (570 ml)
1 cup sugar (225 g) • 1 lemon
3 4" sprigs fresh mint (10 cm) or 1 1/2 teaspoons dried (1.5 g)
6 firm pears with stems
6 ounces PARMIGIANO-REGGIANO, in large nuggets (170 g)
6 sprigs fresh mint for garnish (optional)

In a saucepan, combine water, wine and sugar. Bring mixture to a boil, stirring until sugar dissolves.

Cut lemon peel into long strips, free of the bitter white pith. Juice the peeled lemon. Add peel, juice and mint to wine mixture. Remove from heat.

Leaving stem attached, peel each pear. Cut a thin slice off each pear bottom and quickly, to avoid discoloration, stand pears upright in wine mixture. Return to medium-high heat and bring to a gentle simmer. Adjust heat so liquid does not boil. Cook pears 15–30 minutes, depending on ripeness. Test regularly with a skewer. When tender throughout, pears are done. Allow pears to cool in poaching liquid for 30 minutes.

Remove pears and strain poaching liquid into a small saucepan. Bring to a boil and cook 15–20 minutes, until it coats a spoon in a light, sticky syrup. If desired, cool syrup and rewarm before serving.

To serve, spoon or brush a small puddle of warm syrup onto each plate. Place a pear in the center and arrange several nuggets of Parmigiano-Reggiano next to it. Garnish with mint sprigs and serve immediately.

Serves 6

Winter

descends upon the fields
and stalls in a soft gray
blanket
of fog. Winter cheese is
very different from the
Parmigiano-Reggiano
made in the other sea-
sons of the year. Inside it
is whiter because the
cows eat dry hay. Softer
and moister, the cheeses
of December, January
and February often
exhibit the flavor and
aroma notes of exotic
fruit and
pineapple. Luscious and
fruity, winter cheese
served in chunks is per-
fect with a flute of
sparkling white wine.

Fettuccine Alfredo
Fettuccine al burro e panna

8 tablespoons unsalted butter (113 g)
1/2 pint heavy cream (118 ml)
1 pound fresh fettuccine (455 g)
1 cup freshly grated PARMIGIANO-REGGIANO (80 g)
Freshly ground pepper
Freshly grated nutmeg

As the water for the pasta first begins to boil, melt the butter in
a large sauté pan over low heat. Add the cream to the butter
and let it warm.
At the same time, salt the pasta water and cook the fresh pasta
until al dente.
Drain the pasta and mix thoroughly with the butter and cream,
keeping the sauté pan over low heat. Add the Parmigiano-
Reggiano and toss until sauce thickens slightly. Season with
fresh pepper and nutmeg.
Remove from the heat and serve immediately with additional
grated Parmigiano-Reggiano at the table.
Serves 4-6

Pasta and Chick-Pea Soup

Pasta e ceci

The Vegetarian Soupbone

Once you've finished chunking and slivering and grating, save the rind. It's just the hardened outer shell of the cheese, so it's completely edible. Then when you are making minestrone or a hearty sauce, toss in a rind. Allow it to flavor the food as it cooks. Once it has softened, remove the leathery rind, cut it into bean-size pieces, and return it to the pot to add surprising cheesy tidbits to your finished dish.

❧

1/8 pound prociutto or ham (57 g) • 1 small red onion
1 medium carrot • 1 stalk celery • 1 large clove garlic
1 1/2 teaspoons rosemary (3 g) • 1/4 cup olive oil (71 ml)
1 28-ounce can plum tomatoes (794 g)
2 15-ounce cans chick-peas (425 g) • 4 cups chicken broth (946 ml)
1 tablespoon tomato paste (11 g) • 1 bay leaf
1 4"-square piece of PARMIGIANO-REGGIANO rind (10 cm)
Salt and pepper to taste • 1 cup small pasta tubes (113 g)

Finely chop together prosciutto or ham, red onion, carrot, celery, garlic and rosemary. Set a 3-quart (3-liter) soup kettle over medium heat. Add olive oil and the chopped mixture and cook 10 minutes until vegetables are softened.

Place tomatoes and their juice into a food processor and chop coarsely. Add to the sautéed vegetables along with the drained chick-peas, chicken broth, tomato paste, bay leaf and Parmigiano-Reggiano rind. Add salt and pepper to taste and stir.

Simmer soup for 30 minutes, stirring occasionally. Remove the softened Parmigiano-Reggiano rind, cut it into 1/4" (0.64 cm) cubes and return to soup. (Soup can be made ahead to this point)

Just before serving, add pasta to simmering soup. When pasta is al dente, ladle soup into bowls and sprinkle generously with freshly grated Parmigiano-Reggiano. Serve immediately. *Serves 4-6*

Roman Semolino Gnocchi

Gnocchi alla romana

4 cups milk (945 ml) • 6 tablespoons unsalted butter, divided (85 g)
1 teaspoon salt (6 g) • 1/4 teaspoon pepper
1/4 teaspoon freshly grated nutmeg
1 cup semolino (113 g) • 1 extra-large egg, beaten
1 cup freshly grated
PARMIGIANO-REGGIANO, divided (80 g)
Vegetable oil

Combine milk, 2 tablespoons (28 g) of the butter, salt, pepper and nutmeg in a large saucepan. Bring almost to a boil. Slowly pour in semolino, stirring constantly to prevent lumps. Lower heat; simmer 3–5 minutes until mixture is thick and pulls away from the sides of the pan. Remove from heat. Mix in egg and 3/4 cup (60 g) of Parmigiano-Reggiano.

Lightly oil a smooth work surface. Spread mixture quickly with oiled spatula to an even thickness of 3/8″ (1 cm). Cool 15 minutes.

Cut into discs with an oiled 2″ (5 cm) round biscuit cutter, using scraps until the mixture is gone. Melt remaining 4 tablespoons (57 g) of butter to brush inside of one large or four individual gratin dishes. Arrange semolino gnocchi as pictured. Brush with remaining melted butter and sprinkle with remaining Parmigiano-Reggiano. (Can be made ahead to this point. Cover and refrigerate)

Preheat oven to 375° F (190° C). Bake 30 minutes, then broil 6″ (15 cm) from heat source until golden. Remove from oven. Let stand 2 minutes to set. Serve hot. *Serves 4*

Rustic Parmigiano-Reggiano Cheese Torte

Torta rustica al formaggio Parmigiano-Reggiano

2 tablespoons unsalted butter (28 g)
1 clove garlic, minced
1/2 cup plain breadcrumbs (57 g)
3/4 cup walnuts, finely chopped (85 g)
1/4 teaspoon salt
1 pound cream cheese, softened (455 g)
1/2 pound grated
PARMIGIANO-REGGIANO (225 g)

2 large egg yolks, whites reserved
1/4 cup + 1 tablespoon heavy cream (20 ml)
2 teaspoons Dijon mustard (12 g)
1/2 teaspoon white pepper
1 tablespoon cornstarch (8 g)
1 1/2 tablespoons finely minced shallots (15 g)
2 egg whites (reserved above)
Pinch cream of tartar

Grease the inside of an 8″ (20 cm) springform pan. Set aside. Preheat oven to 325° F (160° C).

To make crust, melt butter in large sauté pan. Add garlic. Cook briefly. Add breadcrumbs, walnuts and salt. Stir, making sure butter and crumbs are well mixed. Cool. Press mixture into bottom of prepared springform pan.

Blend cream cheese and Parmigiano-Reggiano until smooth. Add egg yolks 1 at a time, until blended. Blend in cream. Add mustard, pepper, cornstarch and minced shallots. Blend until smooth.

In another mixing bowl, beat egg whites with cream of tartar until stiff but not dry. Fold gently into cheese mixture. Spoon into pan and even the surface.

Bake 1 hour. Turn oven off and leave cake inside without opening oven door for 1 hour. Then remove cheesecake and cover with a damp towel. Cool to room temperature.

Glazed Fruit Topping

2 tablespoons unsalted butter (28 g)
2 shallots, minced
1 small tart green apple, sliced with peel
6 dried figs, quartered or sliced (113 g)

Zest of 1 orange and juice of 1/2 the orange
1/3 cup chopped walnuts (43 g)
1/3 cup dried cherries (43 g)
1/3 cup apple jelly (70 g)

Melt butter in a sauté pan and sauté the minced shallots until soft. Add the apples, figs, orange zest, orange juice, walnuts and cherries and simmer on low until the apples are just tender. Spoon topping over cheesecake.

Heat apple jelly in a small pan set over low until just melted. Brush jelly over fruit to add shine. Serve at room temperature. *Serves 12*

Orange, Beet and Parmigiano-Reggiano Salad

Insalata di arance, barbabietole e Parmigiano-Reggiano

1 pound beets, cooked and sliced (455 g)
3 oranges, peeled and sliced
1/3 cup walnuts (35 g)
3 tablespoons orange juice (45 ml)
1 teaspoon lemon juice (5 ml)
1/4 teaspoon salt
3 tablespoons walnut oil or extra-virgin olive oil (45 ml)
2 ounces PARMIGIANO-REGGIANO (57 g)
Freshly ground pepper

Pat beets dry. Arrange beets and orange slices in an attractive overlapping pattern on a large serving platter or on individual plates.

Toast walnuts in a preheated 350° F (175° C) oven until light golden brown, about 10 minutes. Chop finely and sprinkle over the beets and oranges.

Whisk together orange juice, lemon juice and salt. Add oil in a thin, steady stream, whisking constantly. Pour dressing over salad.

Make 1/2 cup (57 g) of thin slivers of Parmigiano-Reggiano with a vegetable peeler. Scatter over the salad. Season with pepper and serve immediately. *Serves 6*